Where Do Insects Live?

Molly Aloian

🜨 Crabtree Publishing Company

www.crabtreebooks.com

Author
Molly Aloian

Publishing plan research and development
Reagan Miller, Crabtree Publishing Company

Editorial director
Kathy Middleton

Editor
Crystal Sikkens

Proofreader
Kelley McNiven

Indexer
Wendy Scavuzzo

Design
Samara Parent

Photo research
Crystal Sikkens

Production coordinator and prepress technician
Samara Parent

Print coordinator
Margaret Amy Salter

Illustrations
Jeannette McNaughton-Julich: page 17

Photographs
Dreamstime: front cover (top left)
Thinkstock: pages 1, 4 (top left), 7, 14 (center), 16 (left), 21, 22
Wikimedia Commons: Aviv Gilad: page 8 (left); Franco Folini: page 8 (right); Docleur Cosmos: page 10; Charlotte Simmonds: page 11; Waugsberg: page 15 (bottom); Carlos Ponte: page 16 (right); Hans Hillewaert: page 19
All other images by Shutterstock

Library and Archives Canada Cataloguing in Publication

Aloian, Molly, author
    Where do insects live? / Molly Aloian.

(Insects close-up)
Includes index.
Issued in print and electronic formats.
ISBN 978-0-7787-1280-0 (bound).--ISBN 978-0-7787-1284-8 (pbk.).--
ISBN 978-1-4271-9366-7 (pdf).--ISBN 978-1-4271-9362-9 (html)

        1. Insects--Habitat--Juvenile literature. 2. Insects--Habitations--
Juvenile literature. I. Title.

QL467.2.A565 2013   j595.7   C2013-904042-0
                                       C2013-904043-9

Library of Congress Cataloging-in-Publication Data

Aloian, Molly.
  Where do insects live? / Molly Aloian.
    p. cm. -- (Insects close-up)
  Includes an index.
  ISBN 978-0-7787-1280-0 (reinforced library binding) -- ISBN 978-0-7787-
1284-8 (pbk.) -- ISBN 978-1-4271-9366-7 (electronic pdf) -- ISBN 978-1-4271-
9362-9 (electronic html)
  1. Insects--Habitat--Juvenile literature. I. Title. II. Series: Aloian, Molly.
Insects close-up.

  QL467.2.A448 2013
  595.7--dc23
                                       2013023438

Crabtree Publishing Company

www.crabtreebooks.com   1-800-387-7650

Printed in Hong Kong/092013/BK20130703

Published in Canada
Crabtree Publishing
616 Welland Ave.
St. Catharines, Ontario
L2M 5V6

Published in the United States
Crabtree Publishing
PMB 59051
350 Fifth Avenue, 59th Floor
New York, New York 10118

Published in the United Kingdom
Crabtree Publishing
Maritime House
Basin Road North, Hove
BN41 1WR

Published in Australia
Crabtree Publishing
3 Charles Street
Coburg North
VIC 3058

Contents

What is an insect?

An insect is an animal. It is an **invertebrate**. An invertebrate is an animal that does not have a **backbone**. A backbone is a group of bones down the middle of an animal's back. Insects belong to a big group of invertebrates called **arthropods**.

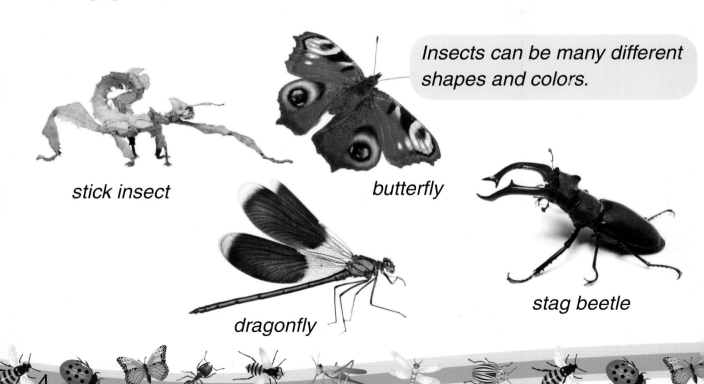

Insects can be many different shapes and colors.

stick insect

butterfly

dragonfly

stag beetle

4

Awesome armor

Instead of a backbone, an insect has a hard covering over its entire body, even its head and legs. This hard covering is called an **exoskeleton**. It protects the insect's body like a suit of armor.

An exoskeleton is waterproof. This means water cannot get through to the insect's body underneath.

Insects everywhere!

Insects can live almost everywhere. Most insects live in warm, damp **habitats**. A habitat is the natural place where an animal lives. Some insect habitats can be underground, in swamps, forests, or even your backyard!

Many different insects live in this forest habitat.

Habitat homes

Habitats provide insects with everything they need to stay alive, such as water, food, space, and the right temperatures. Insects can also find homes in their habitats. Homes protect insects from **predators** and bad weather. Some insects find a home on plants or between rocks. Others build their homes.

A butterfly might find a home in a tree or bush.

Living underground

Some insects make homes called **burrows** in underground habitats. Burrows are tunnels dug into the ground. Most insects that dig burrows are **solitary** insects. Solitary insects live alone. Certain types of beetles, crickets, and wasps are solitary insects.

burrow

The Jerusalem cricket is a solitary insect. It comes out of its burrow at night to look for plants to eat.

Keep out!

Solitary insects make **narrow** burrows so predators cannot get in. Predators are animals that hunt and eat other animals. Solitary wasps are predators. They hunt other insects in their habitats. Once a wasp catches an insect, it brings the insect back to its burrow to eat.

This solitary wasp is carrying a fly into its burrow to eat.

fly

What do you think?

Ants live in **colonies**, or groups, underground. Is an ant a solitary insect? Why or why not?

Wood burrows

Some insects, including carpenter bees, dig burrows into trees or wood. These insects have strong jaws that can cut through hard tree bark and wood. They chew through the wood to make rooms to live in.

Carpenter bees do not eat the wood when chewing through it.

Dead wood

Some female beetles dig small burrows into fallen trees and dead logs. They lay eggs inside the burrows. Babies, called **larvae**, hatch from the eggs and feed on the wood. The larvae make more burrows in the wood as they eat. The larvae stay in the burrows until they become adults.

beetle larvae

11

What do you think?

Do both carpenter bees and beetle larvae eat the wood as they are making their burrows?

Living in large groups

Some insects are **social** insects. Social insects live in large groups. The groups are called colonies. Some colonies have over one million insects. Ants, honeybees, and termites are social insects.

Queen termites make the babies in a colony. They are much larger than the other termites.

queen termite

This ant nest has many babies in it. The baby ants are white and orange.

What do you think?

How is a colony of social insects like a **community** of people?

Working together

Many social insects, such as honeybees and wasps, build homes called **hives** or nests. They work together to protect their homes from predators. Social insects also raise baby insects and store food in their homes. Working together helps these insects stay alive.

Honeybee hives

An entire colony of honeybees live together in a hive.

Honeybees are social insects that live in hives. Their hives are made of **beeswax**. Beeswax is a substance that honeybees make inside their bodies. It comes out of their bodies in flakes.

Making cells

The bees use their legs and **mouthparts** to soften the flakes of wax. They can then shape the wax into small **cells**. A cell is a six-sided space inside a hive. Some cells contain food such as honey and **nectar**. Bees collect nectar from flowers in their habitats.

Some cells in a hive contain eggs and larvae.

cell

larva

egg

Nest builders

Some social insects build nests big enough for a large group. Most ants build their nests by removing dirt or sand from underground. They carry the dirt from inside their nest and pile it outside. This creates **anthills**.

Some anthills are big, others are small.

Tunnels and rooms

The nests of both ants and termites are full of winding tunnels with many rooms. The rooms are used for protecting eggs and larvae, and storing food. Some ant and termite nests have rooms for growing **fungi**. Ants and termites grow fungi for food.

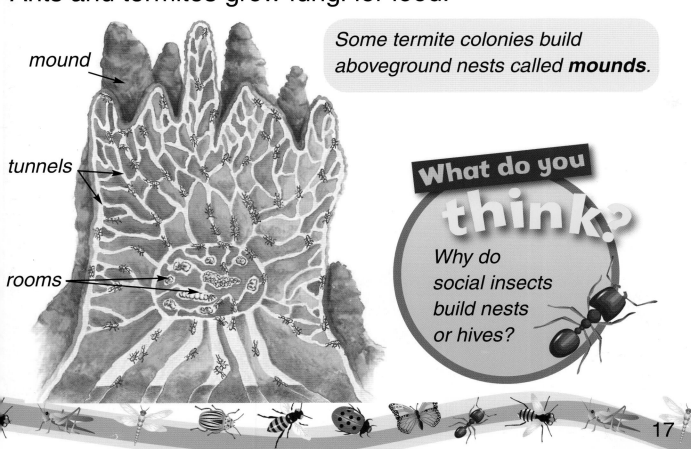

mound

tunnels

rooms

Some termite colonies build aboveground nests called **mounds**.

What do you think?

Why do social insects build nests or hives?

In water

Some insects live in or on water, such as lakes, ponds, swamps, or streams. Most of these insects hatch from eggs and spend the first part of their lives underwater. As adults, these insects may leave the water to live on land, but they are never far from their water habitat.

A mosquito lives underwater until it becomes an adult.

adult mosquito

mosquito larva underwater

Legs like paddles

Water striders are insects that live on water. They use their long back legs like paddles to move themselves across the water. They use their short front legs to catch and eat other insects that are on the water's surface.

long legs

short legs

What do you think?

Is a water strider a predator? Why or why not?

Protecting insects

Insects have the water, food, temperatures, and space they need to survive in their habitats. If those habitats change or become unclean, insects may not survive. Insects are food for many other animals. Without insects, these animals may not survive either.

Garbage, chemicals, and other pollution can harm insect habitats and threaten the lives of insects.

Clean up!

You can help save insects by keeping the environment clean. Get your family, friends, and neighbors to help, too. Ask people to use fewer chemicals and stop using **pesticides** on their gardens and lawns.

Ask your family and friends to help pick up garbage in your neighborhood.

In-depth insects

This activity will show your family and friends what you've learned about insects. Choose an insect from this book or research one on the internet. Draw a picture of the insect and write down everything you've learned about it. The questions below may help you.

What habitat does the insect live in?
Does the insect live on or in water?
Does the insect live in a nest, burrow, or a hive?
Is the insect social or solitary?

Learning more

Books

Green, Jen. *Incredible Insects: An Amazing Insight into the Lives of Ants, Termites, Bees and Wasps*. Armadillo Publishing, 2013.

Spilsbury, Richard and Louise A. Spilsbury. *Ant Colonies* (Animal Armies). PowerKids Press, 2013.

Kalman, Bobbie. *The ABCs of Insects* (ABCs of the Natural World). Crabtree Publishing Company, 2009.

Kalman, Bobbie and John Crossingham. *Insect Homes* (The World of Insects). Crabtree Publishing, 2005.

Websites

Insect Habitats: The Nature Conservancy
www.nature.org/newsfeatures/specialfeatures/animals/insects/index.htm

Fun Insect Facts for Kids—Interesting information about Insects
www.sciencekids.co.nz/sciencefacts/animals/insect.html

Let's Talk About Insects
http://urbanext.illinois.edu/insects/01.html

National Geographic Kids: Honeybees
http://kids.nationalgeographic.com/kids/animals/creaturefeature/honeybees

Words to know

Note: Some boldfaced words are defined where they appear in the book.

fungi (FUHN-guy) noun Plantlike living things

larvae (LAHR-vee) noun Baby insects that hatch from eggs

mouthparts (MOUTH-pahrts) noun Body parts that insects use to gather or eat food

narrow (NAR-oh) adjective Describing something that is of less than usual width

nectar (NEK-ter) noun A sweet liquid found in flowers

pesticides (PES-tuh-sahyds) noun Chemicals used to kill insects

predators (PRED-uh-ters) noun Animals that hunt other animals for food

social (SOH-shul) adjective Describing animals that live in groups

solitary (SOL-i-ter-ee) adjective Describing animals that live alone

A noun is a person, place, or thing. An adjective is a word that tells you what something is like. A verb is an action word that tells you what someone or something does.

Index